C000063532

DUMFRIES AND GALLOWAY INDEPENDENTS

DAVID DEVOY

AMBERLEY

First published 2017

Amberley Publishing
The Hill, Stroud
Gloucestershire, GL5 4EP

www.amberley-books.com

Copyright © David Devoy, 2017

The right of David Devoy to be identified as
the Author of this work has been asserted in
accordance with the Copyrights, Designs and
Patents Act 1988.

ISBN 978 1 4456 6435 4 (print)
ISBN 978 1 4456 6436 1 (ebook)

All rights reserved. No part of this book may be
reprinted or reproduced or utilised in any form
or by any electronic, mechanical or other means,
now known or hereafter invented, including
photocopying and recording, or in any information
storage or retrieval system, without the permission
in writing from the Publishers.

British Library Cataloguing in Publication Data.
A catalogue record for this book is available from
the British Library.

Origination by Amberley Publishing.
Printed in the UK.

Setting the Scene

Dumfries and Galloway is one of thirty-two unitary council areas of Scotland and is located in the western part of the Southern Uplands. It comprises the historic county of Dumfriesshire as well as the Stewartry of Kirkcudbright and Wigtownshire – the latter two of which are collectively known as Galloway. The administrative centre is the town of Dumfries.

Following the 1975 reorganisation of local government in Scotland, the three counties were joined to form a single region of Dumfries and Galloway, with four districts within it. To the north, Dumfries and Galloway borders East Ayrshire, South Ayrshire and South Lanarkshire; in the east is the Borders and to the south the county of Cumbria in England and the Solway Firth. To the west lies the Irish Sea. The population is around 147,000.

The main rail line from Dumfries railway station via Newton Stewart to Stranraer Harbour railway station was closed under the Beeching cuts. The line previously connected London Euston and the West Coast Main Line with the ferries to Larne Harbour railway station and the Port of Belfast. The Beeching Axe cutting the Castle Douglas & Dumfries Railway and Portpatrick & Wigtownshire Railway has resulted in adverse mileage to connect Stranraer with a longer line via Kilmarnock and Ayr.

The major bus operator in the region was the Caledonian Omnibus Company, formed in 1927 by the British Automobile Traction Company. BAT were the bus-operating division of the British Electric Traction Group, who operated tramcars throughout the UK. Caledonian took over five existing bus companies and over the years added many more through a series of acquisitions. Most of the share capital was taken up by BAT and Thomas Tilling, who owned around 1,000 more shares than BAT. May 1928 saw the company name formally changed to BAT & Tilling Co. Ltd, with the chairmanship alternating each year. This was wound up in 1942 when both companies decided to go their own way, and each subsidiary was allocated to one or other company. Caledonian became a Tilling subsidiary.

A significant event occurred in 1948, when the SMT Group sold out to the British Transport Commission. This brought Caledonian into the same government ownership as its northern rival and neighbour Western SMT. It was decided to merge the two companies under the Western SMT name and management in 1949, as Caledonian was the only major BTC-owned company north of the border along with the SMT Group.

Few independents that operated services had survived in the area, and of those that did, operations were on a small scale. Clarke of Glencaple sold out to Western SMT in 1965 and Murray of Stranraer in 1966. Survivors included Leith of Sanquhar, Blue Band of Lockerbie, Gibson's of Moffat and Carruthers of New Abbey.

Others survived, on private hire work and school contracts. It was only when a change in the law occurred in October 1986, and local bus services were de-regulated, that newcomers could enter the market. The new Act abolished road service licensing and allowed for the introduction of competition on local bus services for the first time since the 1930s. To operate a service, all an accredited operator was required to do was provide fifty-six days' notice to the Traffic Commissioner of their intention to commence, cease or alter operation on a route. Another facet was that tendered journeys had to be put out to tender. This was especially relevant in the D&G region as only six services are commercially viable.

Steele's of Lockerbie quickly registered a Dumfries circular service, but it never started. Meanwhile, MacEwan's of Dumfries took over 'The Beef Tub Run', which was a weekend service linking Dumfries and Edinburgh via Moffat that had previously been jointly run by Eastern Scottish and Western SMT. Dickson's of Dumfries won some tendered work around Dumfries while Western launched a shopper's service in direct competition with Gibson's, although it ran only once a day in each direction between Moffat and Dumfries. Gibson's took over the Dumfries Rail Link, which ran as a circular service linking the Whitesands to the railway station, although it later passed to MacEwan's. A new operator, Dumfries & Galloway Minibuses, based in Dalbeattie, began in June 1987 and served six routes in the area. All services were registered commercially and a fleet of four brand-new Freight Rovers were bought to work them. Further tenders were obtained in 1987 by Dickson's, while Nelson of Thornhill won journeys between Dumfries and Sanquhar. Dickson's started a Lochside service in Dumfries on a twenty-minute headway, and no fares were charged for the first two months. Peacock's lost journeys to Shawhead Village, but won more from Dumfries to Moniaive.

It was a constant battle to retain work, but at the end of 1988 Dumfries & Galloway Minibuses ceased trading after sustaining heavy losses. Peacock's won tendered journeys between Dumfries and Thornhill. Leith gained the Sanquhar to Wanlockhead service, while Creighton took the Lockerbie to Borland service over from Rae of Borland. W. J. Gallagher, trading as Annan Minibus Service, provided journeys between Annan and Gretna via Eastriggs. MacEwan's steadily gained more work and in the north of the region Irvine's of Glenluce won some work around Stranraer. McCulloch gained services between Stranraer and Glenluce, while King's of Kirkcowan gained work around Stranraer. Western lost work in the Annan area to Dickson's in October 1988, but chose to keep running the services commercially. The Saturday service linking Lockerbie and Borland passed from Creighton's to J. M. Richardson of Lockerbie, only to be returned at the next re-tendering. King's won services around Newton Stewart, Port William and Isle of Whithorn. Western suffered a great loss in 1989 when Dickson's won thirty contracts out of a total of seventy put out for tender and had to increase their fleet from fourteen to thirty almost overnight. Another casualty was Little's of Annan, who ceased trading in October 1989 after losing all their school contracts to Dickson's. Little's had a fleet of nine smart coaches and had been in business for thirty-two years. Peacock's lost out to both Dickson's and Western SMT, even losing their original service purchased with the Carruthers business, and tried to sell the business. Gibson's suffered competition from Creighton's on their traditional Moffat to Dumfries route. Carnochan of Lockerbie obtained a local route serving Hightae and Templand, as well as journeys around Eaglesfield and Annan. Dickson's crashed in spectacular style and ceased trading overnight in May 1991. The fleet had reached a total of around three dozen, but the receivers were called in after costs spiralled out of control with fuel rising due to the Gulf Crisis. Western regained most of the work. The Dumfries to Stranraer route was jointly operated by McCulloch and MacEwan's from 12 May. Nelson's extended his network to include New Cumnock and MacEwan's gained more work in the Stewartry. Ownership of Creighton's of Lockerbie changed in April 1991 when Agnes Proudfoot sold the business to Steele's of Lockerbie. Even Western Scottish (as Western SMT had become) returned to the private sector in 1991 after the Scottish Bus Group was sold to its management.

By 1994, Anderson's of Langholm, Houston's Minicoaches and Carmichael of Lockerbie had joined the fray with some tendered services. Nelson's of Thornhill withdrew from all service work at the end of July. The mighty Stagecoach entered the area in 1994 with a £6 million takeover of Western. A new operator, Galloway of Port William, began operating between Port William and Kirkcudbright but didn't last long. Meanwhile, MacEwan's purchased the Peacock business in the summer of 1995. A new venture for the company was the introduction of an open-top tour of Dumfries, launched in July 1996 to coincide with the bicentenary of Robert Burns, which ran five times daily. Significant expansion was also won when they were awarded the Borders Rail Link service, which connected Galashiels to Carlisle. This contract was paid one third by D&G Council and the rest by Borders Council. Sadly, Leith of Sanquhar ceased running buses in 1997, although the company was not officially wound up for another two years.

1998 saw MacEwan's win the prestigious 'Solway Clipper' service, which linked Dumfries and Stranraer over a 75-mile route, and three brand-new coaches were purchased and branded for this service. The company was only founded in 1985 and had by 1998 a £1.4 million turn-over, a fleet of thirty-eight vehicles and fifty-two employees. The former Carruthers livery made a comeback when MacEwan's painted a few buses with the fleetname 'Dumfries and District'. A new name appeared the following year when McCall's of Lockerbie introduced a long-lost route linking Moffat and Galashiels with help from the Rural Transport Fund. Anderson's of Langholm won service 124, which connected Langholm and Samye Ling, and 127, which went from Langholm to Newcastleton. King's of Kirkcowan won more routes around Whithorn, Stranraer and Newton Stewart. Steele's Coaches had been reconstituted in 1996, but had to call in the receivers in early 1999. A new kid on the block appeared in Annan, when Cuthbert Ralston, trading as Oor Taxi, obtained a few journeys on local services. December 1999 saw Gibson's of Moffat bow out of operating service work; the firm had been running since 1919, but the loss of certain school contracts that were tied in with the service made it uneconomical to continue although private hire work would continue.

The new century saw the establishment of a new company. Dave Garnett had owned ABC Travel of Southport, but had sold the business the previous year. His new operation was called White Star of Lockerbie, and won a five-year contract to run service 382, which linked Carlisle to Moffat via Lockerbie. Four brand-new buses were purchased for the route. A further service linking Biggar and Lockerbie followed and others were gained as time went by.

May 2003 saw Stagecoach make some gains when it was announced that White Star of Lockerbie had been purchased. The prestigious Stranraer to Dumfries service was won back on re-tendering, but a few services went the other way in 2004, with Armstrong of Castle Douglas gaining the Dumfries to Thornhill route and Houston's gained a couple of ex-White Star routes in the Lockerbie area, which Stagecoach wished to discontinue. April 2006 saw King's of Kirkcowan gaining control of Armstrong's of Castle Douglas, which now traded as ABC Travel. The following year began with two 'bus wars'. MacEwan's lost most of its D&G tenders, but would continue to run commercially on the Dumfries to Kirkcudbright service a few minutes ahead of the Western service, provided under contract.

Western's associated company Schoolbus Scotland registered the route just in front of MacEwan's, leading to the inevitable result that MacEwan's pulled out. Fortunately the company retained the Dumfries to Edinburgh service. The second involved King's of Kirkcowan who won the tender for the X75 Stranraer to Dumfries route, but Western registered the service commercially. King's gained some work and vehicles however when Kiwi Coaches of Newton Stewart ceased. They also won a five-year contract to operate the Newton Stewart to Girvan route.

2008 saw Gibson's of Moffat cease running coaches due to an increase in the price of fuel affecting profit margins. The following year saw MacEwan's set up 'MacEwan's Passenger Services', which was a separate company based in Jedburgh to operate the Kelso to Hawick service. Oor Coaches lost the Annan Circular in March, but Houston's gained the Dumfries to Thornhill, Annan to Newbie and Lochmaben to Lockerbie Industrial Estate routes. A new development in 2010 saw SWESTRANS (the South West of Scotland Transport Partnership) provide vehicles to successful tender winners, in the new SWESTRANS colours of light green and purple. Houston's were among the first to benefit when they won routes in the Annan and Lockerbie areas. Oor Coaches won service 385, linking Dumfries and Annan, and MacEwan's won back the Dumfries to New Abbey and Dalbeattie routes. Three buses received the old Carruthers brown and yellow colours to work these, but with MacEwan's fleet names. In the event, however, the services barely lasted for three months and were cancelled after the company's vehicle authorisation was cut from forty to thirty-two vehicles.

April 2011 saw the closure of the Jedburgh outstation after Firstbus registered the Hawick to Kelso route commercially and the tender was cancelled. McCall's won the Lockerbie to Corrie Common and Lockerbie town service from Houston's. Changes in the Stranraer area saw King's lose the Stranraer to Portpatrick and Newton Stewart to Portpatrick tenders, but won Stranraer to Kirkcolm and Stranraer to Wigton services to compensate. Houston's obtained the Dumfries to Dalbeattie, and Dumfries to Thornhill services. McCulloch took on the weekday service linking Stranraer to Dumfries College.

November 2013 saw MacEwan's lose the Annan/Edinburgh/Dumfries to Biggar services to Stagecoach. This was at the instigation of SPT after a bus had crashed in November 2012. This led to a public inquiry, at which SPT was widely criticised. Meanwhile, McLean's of Stranraer put a diesel-electric Hybrid Optare Solo, funded under the Scottish Green Bus Fund, onto the Cairnryan to Stranraer service.

King's of Kirkcowan applied to increase their ABC fleet by twenty vehicles, but got embroiled with the Traffic Commissioners in a dispute over financial standing. King's and ABC Travel had their licences revoked, but continued to run under appeal. After a public inquiry they were finally revoked in July 2014, and many vehicles were sold to MacEwan's. Robert Armstrong Coaches of Castle Douglas purchased many ex-King and ABC Travel vehicles, but was disqualified from the bus industry after being found guilty of assisting King/ABC Travel to remain in business. Irvine's of Glenluce also surrendered their licences. Houston's steadily increased their fleet, which was now around forty vehicles, operating from the brand-new depot in Lockerbie that had replaced premises rented from Matt Turnbull, the former owner of Blue Band Motors.

No doubt more changes will happen in the future. Operators have come and gone but it has always been interesting. I dedicate this book to all Dumfries and Galloway busmen, many who have helped me over the years, often slowing down for a picture to be taken, moving a vehicle into the sun, or just giving me information. I salute you.

CCK 636 was a Leyland Titan PD2/3/Burlingham L27/26R purchased new by Ribble as their fleet number 2648 in October 1948. On disposal in June 1960 it passed to Carruthers of New Abbey, and was loading at the Whitesands in Dumfries after being pressed into service in Ribble livery. It would run for just over four years before passing to a Glasgow building contractor.

JUT 946E was a Bedford VAM/Willowbrook DP45F purchased new by Gibson of Barlestone in March 1967 as their number 66. It had joined the fleet of Matt Turnbull of Lockerbie by the time of this shot in June 1972. It was captured outside The Rex Cinema in Lockerbie where *Virgin Soldiers* was playing. Blue Band Motors also ran a haulage fleet for many years and had a few depots spread throughout the country but sadly it went bust.

JRB 741N was a Leyland Leopard PSU3C/4R/Duple Dominant E Type B53F purchased new by Nottingham City Transport as their 741 in July 1975. It was one of a pair purchased by Graham's of Paisley in August 1981 and was sent to Duple at Barrhead to have a new front end fitted, including a Bristol Dome to house the destination screen. It would remain in the fleet until April 1990 when it was acquired by Gibson's of Moffat, and is seen near Ae village.

T76 JBA is a Dennis Dart SLF/Plaxton Pointer B29F that was new to Rai of Birmingham in June 1999. It has also served with Pete's Travel, Epsom Buses and D&G Council before reaching McCall's of Lockerbie. It was working on service 512, which is the Castle Douglas town service previously operated by ABC Travel.

TNB 448K was a Seddon Pennine 6/Plaxton Elite C51F purchased new by SELNEC PTE as their number 247 in June 1972. Brownrigg's of Thornhill acquired it from Gibson's of Hamilton in 1979. The Seddon Pennine 6 was a front-engined chassis with a Perkins engine.

EN 8540 was a Leyland Titan PD1/Roe H31/25R purchased new by Bury Corporation as their fleet number 106 in March 1946. It was bought from Tiger Coaches (dealer) in 1958, and is seen at Dumfries Whitesands. The company had an office across the road from where tours and private hires were operated. The business and two vehicles were sold to Western SMT in August 1965.

KOG 947P was a Leyland Leopard PSU3C/4R/Plaxton Elite C34F that was new to Bowens of Birmingham in September 1975. It was up-seated to C53F on joining the Carruthers of New Abbey fleet and was the flagship for a number of years. It passed to W. L. & W. Peacock (Truck Services) Ltd, based at Locharbriggs, with the business in December 1983, and is seen on a private hire to Glasgow.

M925 TYG was a Mercedes 0405/Optare Prisma B49F that was built as a demonstrator for Optare, Leeds, in March 1995. It was sold to Skyeways of Kyle of Lochalsh, where it was re-registered as M6 SKY in June 1996. MacEwan's of Dumfries acquired it in June 2000 and it became M211 YAS to allow Skyeways to retain the cherished registration number. It was resold in 2003 to Rapson's of Inverness, where it was given fleet number 199.

BX10 DHK is a BMC Hawk 900 B27F that was delivered new to Houston's of Lockerbie in April 2010 in SWESTRANS livery, but had been re-allocated by the council to Andy McCall and was working on service 112 to Eskdalemuir. SWESTRANS is one of seven Regional Transport Partnerships in Scotland and covers an area contiguous with the boundaries of Dumfries and Galloway Council. The Partnership Board consists of five councillors and two external members, one from Scottish Enterprise and one from NHS Dumfries and Galloway.

PGM 249M was a Bedford YRQ/Duple Dominant C45F purchased new by Central SMT as their fleet number C49 in May 1974. On disposal it joined Creighton's of Moffat, and was captured in Lockerbie. Creighton's were based at Colvin Garage in Lockerbie. By 1994 control had passed to D. A. Steele, with bases at 25 Livingston Place, Lockerbie and St Johns Road, Annan.

This Leyland National LN11351/1R B52F was one of four purchased by Dickson's and came from South Wales. Unfortunately Dickson's collapsed, leaving Western Scottish to pick up the pieces. The Leyland National was an integrally constructed British step-floor single-decker bus that was manufactured in large quantities between 1972 and 1985.

GSU 851T was a Leyland Leopard PSU3C/3R/Alexander T Type C49F purchased new by Central SMT as their T369 in April 1979. It passed to Kelvin Central Buses (2511) in March 1989, and then McColl's Coaches of Balloch in August 1993. Gibson's acquired it in June 1994 for use on school contracts, and it was specially brought out of the depot and posed for my visit. I'd like to thank the Gibson family for their help over many years and it was a sad day when operations ceased in November 2007.

GRS 114E was a Leyland Atlantean PDR1/1/Alexander A Type H43/34F that was new as Aberdeen Corporation number 114 in September 1967. It passed to Grampian Regional Council and was later converted to open-top layout for use on tours and hires. It was acquired by MacEwan's for use on a tour of Dumfries for a while, but sadly it was not profitable.

V974 DRM was a Dennis Dart SLF/ Plaxton Pointer B29F purchased new by Dave Garnett, t/a White Star of Lockerbie, in January 2000. The business was purchased by Stagecoach North West, but later some of it was transferred to Stagecoach Western, including this bus, which was numbered as 33074. In its last year of trading, White Star had a turnover of £500,000.

MSJ 374P was a Seddon Pennine VII/Alexander T Type C49F that was delivered new as Western SMT S2568 in July 1976. It was transferred to Clydeside Scottish in 1985 as their number R902. Note the front lower panels cut away for boarding ferries to and from the Isle of Bute. It later passed to Reilly of Bootle before purchase by Steele's of Lockerbie in 1991.

SF09 LZV was a MAN A22/Wright Meridian purchased new by Whitelaw's of Stonehouse in May 2009. It is seen with subsequent owner Houston's of Lockerbie in Dumfries, operating service 236. The firm began as Houston's Mini Coaches in 1975 as a small family-run business with only a few buses available for private hire, school contracts and local council contracts. Depots are located in Lockerbie and Dumfries and a fleet of around forty vehicles is operated.

SK52 UTT was a Dennis Dart SLF/Plaxton Pointer B37F purchased new by HAD Coaches of Shotts in December 2002. The company collapsed in 2004 and it was purchased by John MacEwan and was caught in Dumfries while working on service 501, bound for Castle Douglas. It then passed to GHA Coaches in July 2007 along with sister vehicle SK52 UTU, which was required for the Line 9 service.

A525 JSW was a Volvo B10M-61/Duple Carribean C51F that was new to Little of Annan in March 1984. It passed to Silver Fox Coaches of Renfrew, then Lochview Coaches of Greenock, where it became RJI 4565 in 1993, before passing to Liddell's of Auchinleck in 1995. It was caught on a football hire to Hampden Park in Glasgow.

G364 NHH was a Leyland Swift LBM6T/2RS/Reebur Harrier C37F purchased new by Irving's of Dalston in October 1989. It was acquired by Ian Creighton, t/a Kian's of Annan, in 1994 and was snapped on a pipe-band hire to Glasgow. It would later become JJZ 4375 with 2Way Travel of Broughton.

YSN 959K was a Ford R192/Plaxton Derwent DP45F purchased new by Green's of Kirkintilloch in November 1971. On disposal in 1975 it passed to F. & T. J. Stoneman of Nandean before purchase by Carruthers of New Abbey in January 1977. It was sold with the business to Peacock's of Locharbriggs in December 1983 and remained until it passed to Steele's of Lockerbie in May 1991. It then ran for Bruce of Longtown until March 1996.

SUR 280R was a Leyland Leopard PSU5A/4R/Plaxton Viewmaster C53F purchased new by Waterhouse of Polegate (37) in April 1977. On disposal it passed to McCulloch of Stranraer before joining Irvines of Law, where it was re-registered as 790 CVD. This was changed on disposal to WGD 791R and sold to Jack Waddell of Lochwinnoch. AB Coaches of Totnes purchased it in March 1989 and it was re-registered yet again to UFH 277.

GNL 842N was a Leyland Leopard PSU3C/4R/Alexander Y Type B62F purchased new by Tyne & Wear PTE (842) in July 1975. On disposal it passed to Holloway's of Scunthorpe, before purchase by Carruthers of New Abbey (3) in April 1983 and it passed with the business to Peacock (Truck Services) in December 1983. It would later see service with Dickson's of Dumfries. The location was Shakespeare Street in Dumfries.

N550 GFS was a Scania K113CRB/Van Hool Alizee C51F purchased new by Mayne's of Buckie in May 1996. It was acquired by McCall's from Bowman's of Burthwaite. It has also worked for NBM of Penrith and has carried the registration numbers YSU 989 and YXI7 923.

D347 CBC was a Mercedes O303/15R C53F purchased new by Hirst of Holmfirth in June 1987. It was re-registered as RIL 7844 in June 2001, before passing to Abbeyways in March 2000 as D930 UTU. This was later changed to SEL 36. It had returned to being D930 UTU by the time it reached R. K. Armstrong of Castle Douglas in 2001 and was snapped at Battlefield in Glasgow.

LTV 740P was a Leyland Leopard PSU3C/4R/Willowbrook B55F that was new as Nottingham City Transport number 740 in December 1975. On disposal in May 1981 it joined Graham's of Paisley as their fleet number S23 before reaching Peacock's of Locharbriggs in July 1984. It then moved locally to Steele's of Kirtlebridge in October 1991 before ending its days providing spares for Aspden's of Blackburn.

MNW 336F was a Leyland Leopard PSU3/4R/Plaxton Panorama C49F purchased new by Wallace Arnold Tours of Leeds in April 1968, though it also spent time with their subsidiary company Woburn Garages (London), t/a Evan Evans. It joined Gibson's of Moffat in January 1978 and remained until October 1983, when it was scrapped.

OSM 95M was a Bedford YRT/Plaxton Derwent B60F purchased new by Matt Turnbull of Lockerbie in November 1973. It had the highest seating capacity of any single-deck service bus in Scotland at the time and was resting at the depot in Lockerbie. It would later run for Gray of Killen, Dew's of Somersham and Athelstan of Malmesbury.

M255 UKX was a Mercedes Urbanranger OH1416/Wright B47F purchased new by University Bus of Hatfield in January 1995. It is seen in Kirkcudbright while working on service 505. The Urbanranger was bodied with Wright Crusader bodywork and was only available from 1995 to 1998. In all, only sixteen were built.

RDC 24H was a Ford R192/Plaxton Elite C45F purchased new by Bob's Buses of Thornaby in February 1970. It is seen with Nithcree Distributers of Lochfoot who ran delivery vans and a couple of coaches. The coaches ceased in 1990 but a driver training school was then operated.

M291 OUR was an Iveco 480-10-21 Turbocity/Wadham Stringer B47F that was built for stock for coach dealer Alan Wilson of Ratby in November 1994. It passed to Mike De Courcey of Coventry before purchase by MacEwan's of Dumfries in 2003, and is shown parked up in Peebles. Only six of this combination were built for the UK market.

USO 177S was a Ford R1114/Alexander Y Type B53F that was new as Alexander (Northern) NT177 in December 1977. It passed to John Nelson of Thornhill in September 1987, and was captured on a dreich day working on the Dumfries to Sanquhar service.

C270 TPL was a Leyland Tiger TRCTL11/3RZ/Plaxton Paramount 3500 C50F purchased new by Safeguard Coaches of Guildford in March 1986. It was re-registered to DSK 560 in September 1993, becoming C933 VPM on disposal. It passed to Allison's, t/a Kiwi, of Newton Stewart and is seen in Glasgow. It reached Riverside Transport and Training of Paisley in 1998, and onwards to DJ International of Barrhead in 1999, becoming RIL 3690 in June 1999.

YJ54 ZXZ is an Optare Solo M850 B26F purchased new by Houston of Lockerbie in February 2005, captured as it arrives in Dumfries while working on service 504 to Lochfoot.

S51 RGA was a MAN 11.220/Marshall B36F that was new as Dart Buses of Paisley number A50 in January 1999. On the demise of Dart, it passed to MacEwan's of Dumfries in 2001 and was captured at Catherinefield. It would see further service with Coachcare Travel of Leicester.

K185 YDW was an Optare MetroRider MR01 B31F purchased new by Cardiff Transport as their fleet number 185 in August 1992. It was acquired by White Star and is seen on the forecourt of Central Garage in Lockerbie. In its last year of trading White Star had a turnover of £500,000, but it sadly sold out to Stagecoach (North West).

SJS 36L was a Ford R1014/Willowbrook B56F purchased new by Newton's of Dingwall for use on oil-related contracts in July 1973. It became number 9 in the fleet of Carruthers of New Abbey in January 1976, and would stay until December 1983 when it passed to Peacock's of Locharbriggs with the business.

K813 HUM was a Volvo B10M-60/Van Hool Alizee C48Ft that was delivered new to Wallace Arnold Tours of Leeds in March 1993. It became Aberfeldy Motor Services' XSV 893 in February 2000, returning to its original plate a year later. Gibson's of Moffat snapped it up in May 2001 and it ran until March 2002 when it joined I. & C. Creighton, t/a Kian's of Annan. It soon became USV 365, and was snapped on a visit to Edinburgh.

PER 57R was an AEC Reliance 6U3ZR/Plaxton Supreme C57F purchased new by Miller Bros of Foxton in May 1977. It joined McCulloch of Stranraer in 1991 from Smith of High Wycombe, and was working on a school run in Stranraer.

GFM 882 was a Bristol L6A/ECW B35R that was new as Crosville KB73 in April 1948 and was converted to B35F by Crosville for One Man Operation in 1958 as number SLA73. This involved moving the entrance to the front and fitting a slanting window at the side to enable the driver to collect the fares. It passed to Thames Valley as their number 302. John MacEwan purchased it in 1980 from Philip of Dunfermline as a heritage vehicle and it was caught in Dumfries.

R280 EKH was an Optare Excel L1150 B45F purchased new by East Yorkshire as their fleet number 280 in August 1997. It joined McCulloch's of Stranraer in 2002 and is seen in its home town working on service 267, bound for Portpatrick. It later passed to King's of Kirkcowan before export to Lough Rea Hotel, Loughrea, Eire, where it carried the registration number 97-G-20318.

TSJ 77S was a Leyland Leopard PSU3D/4R/Alexander Y Type B53F that was new as Western SMT L2717 in January 1978. It was sold to Maidstone & District as their number 3002 in 1995, then to Wealden Omnibuses of Five Oak, but returned to Scotland with MacEwan's of Dumfries in 1996. It was given the 'Dumfries and District' livery, based on the old Carruthers colours.

E303 FWV was a Scania N112DRB/Van Hool DP44F purchased new by Terminus of Crawley in July 1988. It was acquired by Beeston's of Hadleigh as SJI 4427, before purchase by East Yorkshire as their number 246. It joined King's of Kirkcowan in 2002 and was captured in Newton Stewart working on service 259, bound for Girvan.

GOH 355N was a Leyland PSU3B/4R/Marshall DP49F purchased new by Midland Red as their number 55 in November 1974. It was one of a batch of twelve similar buses and formed part of Midland Red's S28 class. It subsequently passed to Midland Red (South) before purchase by Dumfriesshire independent Gibson's of Moffat. It is seen having just arrived on service at Dumfries Whitesands and had unloaded outside the Western Scottish Office.

WUS 248 was an AEC Reliance 2MU3R/Plaxton Panorama C37F purchased new by Cotter's Tours of Glasgow in May 1959. It was fully refurbished by Cotter's Sales & Service in 1982 for Hope & Ian Brownrigg, and was handed over by company-founder Bernard Cotter himself. It still exists and has changed owners recently, but needs a lot of TLC to restore it once again.

S582 ACT was a Mercedes O814D/Autobus Classique B33F purchased new by Sanders of Holt as their fleet number 158 in March 1999. It joined the fleet of Armstrong of Castle Douglas in 2004 and is shown at Dumfries Whitesands while working a journey to Moniaive.

PY02 KTP was a Dennis Dart SLF/Plaxton Pointer B37F purchased new by White Star of Lockerbie in April 2002, and is seen parked on the forecourt of Central Garage. It passed to Stagecoach Western with the services and became number 33079 in that fleet. On disposal in 2015 it joined the Lanarkshire fleet of JMB Travel, based in Newmains, for a spell, but it has recently been replaced.

K860 PCN was a Dennis Dart 9.8SDL/Wright Handybus B40F that was new as Sunderland & District number 8060 in August 1992. On disposal it passed to Dart Buses of Paisley before reaching MacEwan's in 2001. It would later become Midland Rider of Oldsbury's number 1012.

FDV 823V was a Leyland Leopard PSU3E/4R/Willowbrook 003 C49F purchased new by Western National (3532) in April 1980. It worked for Devon General and City of Oxford before disposal to Vanguard of Bedworth. It joined the Argyll Group in 1990, and moved to John Boyce and Ian MacTavish of Dalmuir before reaching John Nelson's fleet in 1991, and was unloading at Dumfries Whitesands.

UBR 656V was a Leyland Leopard PSU3E/4R/Plaxton Supreme C53F purchased new by Weardale of Frosterley in November 1979. It passed to Irving's of Dalston before reaching Kian's of Annan in August 1996, and was caught on a football hire to Glasgow. It would pass to King's of Kirkcowan in March 1998, and Docherty's of Irvine the following year for use on school contracts.

FNM 865Y was a Leyland Tiger TRCTL11/3R/Plaxton Paramount 3500 C50F purchased new by Armchair of Brentford in April 1983. On disposal it passed to Ivan Jarvis of Maltby, where it was re-registered as JSV 468. It was acquired by Andy McCall in March 2003 and remained until 2006, although it was not scrapped until March 2006.

LAG 287F was a Leyland Leopard PSU3/3R/Northern Counties B53F purchased new by AA Motor Services member Robert Tumilty, Irvine, in June 1968, passing to fellow member Young's of Ayr after Tumilty retired. It was acquired by Leith of Sanquhar in June 1979, and is seen here in its home town. It was resold to Dickson's of Dumfries in September 1983, and later saw service with Webber's of Bilsland.

FSM 419L was a Ford R1114/Duple Dominant Express C49F that was delivered new to Gibson's of Moffat in April 1973, remaining in the fleet until March 1987. The Duple Dominant was coach bodywork built by Duple between 1972 and 1982 and had an all-steel structure. The Ford R-Series was a range of bus and coach chassis that evolved from designs made by Thames Trader until the mid-1960s. A number of components were shared with the D-series lorry, including the vertically mounted engine at the front of the vehicle, ahead of the front axle so as to provide a passenger entrance opposite the driver.

N743 LUS was a Mercedes 709D/Wadham Stringer B29F purchased new by Pathfinder of Newark as their number 7 in October 1995. The use of a Glasgow registration number is explained by being supplied by Glasgow dealer Blythswood Motors. It passed to McLean's of Stranraer for use around the ports of Stranraer and Cairnryan. Stena Line Ferries link Cairnryan to Belfast in Northern Ireland.

B116 KPF was a Leyland Tiger TRCTL11/3RH/Berkhof Everest C49Ft that was new as London Country BTL16 in November 1984. It became Kentish Bus number 20 before purchase by John Nelson of Thornhill in January 1991. It was re-registered as A5 JNC in August 1993, and was snapped at Thornhill. It would pass to Premier Bus & Coach of Blyth in February 1995.

GSU 861T was a Leyland Leopard PSU3C/3R/Alexander (Belfast) B53F that was new as Central SMT number T379 in July 1979. It became Kelvin Central Buses' number 1521 before purchase by Gibson's of Moffat in August 1996, and is seen at the depot. It would remain until sold for scrap to Dunsmore (dealer) of Larkhall in March 2000.

KUX 216W was a Leyland Leopard PSU5D/4R/Duple Dominant III C53F that was new as Whittle of Highley number 16 in November 1980. On disposal it passed to Oare's of Holywell before purchase by John MacEwan in February 1991. It moved to McCulloch's of Stoneykirk, near Stranraer, in February 1992.

GNL 842N was a Leyland Leopard PSU3C/4R/Alexander Y Type B62F purchased new by Tyne & Wear PTE (842) in July 1975. On disposal it passed to Holloway's of Scunthorpe, before purchase by Carruthers of New Abbey (3) in April 1983, and passed with the business to Peacock (Truck Services) in December 1983. It would later see service with Dickson's of Dumfries. The location was Locharbriggs.

B332 LSA was a Leyland Tiger TRCTL11/2RP/Alexander TC Type C47Ft that was new as Northern Scottish NCT32 in January 1995, later being re-registered as TSV 722. It passed to Stagecoach Bluebird with the business becoming number 446. It reverted to its original plate before purchase by MacEwan's of Dumfries from Collison of Stonehouse in March 2002, and was traded in to Wealdon Omnibus (dealer) in July 2004.

CTL 138X was a Leyland Tiger TRCTL11/2R/Plaxton Supreme VI Express C53F purchased new by Hornsby of Ashby in December 1981. It passed to Earnside of Glenfarg and became NHG 550. On disposal it was re-registered as LSL 615X and joined Leith of Sanquhar in February 1989. It remained until 1997 when it passed to Egan Bros Bus Service.

PUH 554R was a Bedford YLQ/Plaxton Supreme C45F purchased new by Hawthorn of Barry in March 1977. It passed to Austin's of Earlston, then Green's of Kirkintilloch, then Hunter of Edinburgh before reaching Creighton's Coaches, and was captured in Lockerbie.

A busy scene in Lockerbie shows Houston's BX10 DHF, a BMC Hawk 225 B45F that was delivered new in April 2010. Hot on its heels is MX10 DXJ, the Hawk, working on service 382. Like other BMC buses, the Hawk is produced in factories in Izmir and is used as a city bus especially in various cities of Israel and Portugal.

A111 SNH was a DAF SB2300/Jonckheere Jubilee P599 C51Ft purchased new by Berryhurst of London in August 1983. It was later re-registered as A2 WCK. John MacEwan purchased it from Sinnamon of Dungannon in August 2000, and resold it to McCall's of Lockerbie four months later. It would remain until scrapped in April 2006.

TGD 763W was a Volvo B10M-61/Van Hool Alizee C40Ft purchased new by Cotter's Coachline of Glasgow in February 1980 for use on their Scotland to London services. It passed to Pride of the Clyde Coaches of Port Glasgow as C50Ft, before reaching James King of Kirkcowan in 1990 and was seen parked beside the River Nith in Dumfries.

SYS 491G was a Bedford VAM/Duple Viceroy C45F purchased new by the Scottish Co-operative for their Majestic Coaches fleet in 1969 and was based at Barrhead depot in Aurs Road. When the fleet was auctioned in 1975 it went to Lockey's of West Auckland and remained there for around four years before sale to Rayner's Coaches of Esh Winning in January 1979. It then joined the fleet of Alan Dickson in early 1982 and was photographed at a rugby international at Edinburgh's Murrayfield Stadium later that year.

SF60 FPY is a MAN A66/MCV Evolution B39F purchased new by Whitelaw of Stonehouse in October 2010. It was one of a pair acquired by McCall's and was leaving Lockerbie for Gretna on service 382. The original name of MAN was 'Maschinenfabrik Augsburg-Nürnberg'. They don't use their full name any more since their headquarters are now in Munich.

DKY 866V was an AEC Reliance 6U3ZR/Plaxton Supreme C53F purchased new by Mosley of Barugh Green in September 1979. It passed to Harris of Catshill before reaching Kiwi in 1991. Kiwi was owned by the Allison Family and were based at Spittal Cottage, Creetown. DKY 866V was on a private hire to Ayr.

L23 WGA was a MAN 11.190/Optare Vecta B42F that was new to Hutchison's of Overtown in October 1993 and lasted in the fleet until May 2000 when it passed to John MacEwan of Dumfries. It moved on again in August 2003 to Moffat & Williamson of Gauldry, then went to Bennett's of Kilwinning and then B&N Coaches of Burnley. It was caught leaving Edinburgh on service 315, bound for Penicuik.

B46 XKJ was a Leyland Tiger TRCTL11/3R/Plaxton Paramount 3500 C53F purchased new by Smith of Sittingbourne in March 1985. It was acquired by Brownrigg's of Thornhill in 1998, and was captured on a visit to Edinburgh. The company began in the 1930s and are still in business today.

UCK 500 was a 1974 Leyland Leopard PSU4B/4RT that was fitted with a Willowbrook Warrior B47F body in June 1989 by Davies Bros of Pencader. It had been new with a Duple C41F body as RBO 194M with Western Welsh (UC474) in February 1974. It was acquired by MacEwan's of Dumfries in September 1999, and is seen about to cross Buccleuch Bridge. It later passed to Choice Buses of Wednesfield as BWP 755M and after running in service for a spell it was cut down as a recovery vehicle for the fleet.

PSM 145S was a Volvo B58-56/Plaxton Supreme C53F purchased new by Little's of Annan in January 1978. It passed to King's of Kirkcowan in 1984 and received a Supreme IV front. Hay's of Huntly acquired it in 1985. Later in its life it became VIW 6244 with Wren of Saltburn.

R28 VSM was a DAF SB3000/Van Hool Alizee C51Ft purchased new by John MacEwan of Amisfield in April 1998 for the Solway Clipper Service, which connected Dumfries and Stranraer. The contract was for five years, but in May 2000 the council decided that they wanted the route to be converted to low-floor operation. The two coaches used on the service were sold to Hutchison's of Overtown. This one later passed to Marbill of Beith, Smith of Coupar Angus and was latterly with Horsburgh of Pumpherston.

MNC 503W was a Leyland Leopard PSU3F/4R/Duple Dominant II C44F purchased new by Greater Manchester PTE subsidiary Charterplan as their number 29 in September 1980. It passed to Freshfields Coaches of Stockport. It joined McCulloch's of Stoneyburn from Rent a Crane, Birmingham, in 1997 and was seen loading in Stranraer for Portpatrick on service 367.

F928 YWY was a Mercedes 811D/Optare StarRider B26F that was new as London Buses' SR28 in November 1988. It passed to the privatised London Central in October 1994, and remained until 1998. It was acquired by MacEwan's of Dumfries in April 2000, and was captured in Southerness. It passed to Meffan of Kirriemuir in April 2001 and was re-registered as TIL 8207, passing with the business to Stagecoach in March 2006 where it received fleet number 41341.

WEB 132T was an AEC Reliance 6U3ZR/Plaxton Supreme III C57F purchased new by Miller's of Foxton in January 1979. It was re-registered as HSV 194, before becoming BEG 866T on disposal. It ran for Premier Travel and then Draper's of Sidcup before joining MacEwan's of Dumfries in March 1998. It was wearing Dumfries & District livery when snapped at Amisfield.

F155 CSM was a very smart Volvo B10M-61/Ikarus Blue Danube C49Ft purchased new by Gibson's of Moffat in May 1989. It was re-registered as HIL 8022 in March 1992, and was captured in Dumfries. It would pass to Smith, t/a Fisher's Tours, of Aberfeldy in February 2001, A1 Minibuses of Methil in February 2006 and GB Resourcing of Birmingham in 2007. It was last licensed in 2010.

HSM 938E was a Bedford SB5/Willowbrook DP29F+Goods purchased new by Matt Turnbull of Lockerbie in February 1967 for the Glasgow to Lockerbie service. It is seen resting in Moffat on 7 July 1971 with a Southern National Bristol RE/ECW parked in the square behind it.

G52 HDW was a Kassbohrer Setra S215HR C49Ft purchased new by Bebb's of Llantwit Fardre in April 1990. It passed to Graham's of Gretna and was working under contract to Wallace Arnold Tours of Leeds when snapped in Glasgow. The name 'Setra' comes from 'selbsttragend' (self-supporting). This refers to the integral nature of the construction of the vehicles back in the 1950s when competitor vehicles still featured a separate chassis and body (often being manufactured by separate companies).

P20 JLS was a Mercedes 711D/Plaxton Beaver C25F purchased new by Leask of Lerwick in March 1997. It passed to ABC Travel of Castle Douglas and was captured in Newton Stewart working on the service to Girvan. The company was incorporated in 2006 and the registered address was 36 Main Street, Kirkcowan, Wigtownshire – the same as James King.

LFJ 850W was a Bristol LHS6L/ECW B35F purchased new by Western National as their number 96 in December 1980. It would move to Thames Transit before being sold to Moffat & Williamson in 1991. It joined MacEwan's of Dumfries in December 1994 and lasted until it was cannibalised for spares in 1998.

A47 GLD was a Neoplan Cityliner N116 C53Ft. R. K. Armstrong of Castle Douglas purchased it from Hasting's of Edinburgh in 1996, and it is seen on a hire to Glasgow. It left the fleet in February 2007 to join Mancini of Faversham. Robert Armstrong sold his business to James King in April 2006.

J411 NCP was a Daf SB220L/Ikarus Citybus B49F J411 NCP purchased new by Liverline of Bootle in July 1992. It passed to Clarkson of South Emsall before reaching MacEwan's of Dumfries in August 2002, and was snapped in Peebles. It passed to Kimes of Folkingham for further service.

XWO 257T was a Bedford YMT/Van Hool McArdle C53F purchased new by Cleverly of Pontypool in January 1979. It passed to King's of Kirkcowan before reaching Brownrigg's of Thornhill in June 1988, and was seen parked by the River Nith in Dumfries.

R828 FSX was a Mercedes O810D/Plaxton Beaver C23F purchased new by Fairline
Coaches of Glasgow in June 1998 for use on the airport service. On disposal in 2002
it passed to James King as a twenty-seven-seater, and was caught passing through
Newton Stewart. Sadly, James King and ABC Travel had their licences revoked
in 2014.

G795 RNC was a Leyland Tiger TRCTL11/3RZ/Duple 320 C53F that was new as
Smith Shearing number 795 in August 1989. It passed to Maidstone & District as
number 2912 and was re-registered as YSU 872. It joined Gordon Bruce of Twynholm
from Hunter's of Sauchie in October 2006 and remained until July 2007, when it
passed to Hayward of Carmarthen.

T399 OWA was a Scania N113DRB/East Lancs Citizen CH78F purchased by Dunn-Line of Nottingham in July 1999, although it is believed to have been a demonstrator. It passed to John MacEwan in 2003 and saw some use on the Dumfries to Edinburgh service. Unfortunately the trees on the route had not been trimmed in years and it was decided that double-deck operation was too dangerous. It was resold to Harrogate Coach Travel, where it would become 5480 WY. It then went to Graham's of Kelvedon, then SBC Leisure.

This 1970 Leyland Leopard PSU3A/4R began life as Midland Red WHA 240H, fitted with Plaxton Panorama coachwork. It was re-bodied in August 1981 with this Duple Dominant body for Lucas of Kingsley Holt and was seen leaving Sanquhar on a journey to Kirkconnel. It ran for Leith of Sanquhar between July 1992 and July 1997 when it passed to Keenan of Coalhall.

UCY 182N was an AEC Reliance 6U3ZR/Duple Dominant C49F purchased new by South Wales Transport (182) in September 1974. It was purchased by Dickson's of Dumfries and is shown in Dumfries, working on a short-lived local service from Kenilworth Road to Queensberry Square, as the company collapsed overnight shortly after.

PVN 314R was a classic combination of AEC Reliance 6MU2R/Plaxton Supreme C49F purchased new by Bob's Buses of Thornaby in January 1977. It was acquired by Little's in April 1977 and is shown on a tour of the capital, looking superb in the salmon and grey livery used by this sadly missed, quality operator, which ceased operations in October 1989.

YJ10 EZA is an Optare Solo M960 B30F purchased new by Alba of Great Salkeld in April 2010. It joined McCall's of Lockerbie in March 2015, and was captured leaving Dumfries on service 385, bound for Annan.

M804 HGB was a Volvo B10M-62/Van Hool Alizee C53F purchased new by Muir of Coalburn in May 1995. It was acquired by Gibson's of Moffat in March 1998 and was re-registered as OIL 2939. It was sold to Robertson of Cuminestown in March 2005 and later saw service with MCT Transport of Motherwell.

L670 PWT was a MAN 11.190/Optare Vecta B40F that was built in April 1994 as an Optare demonstrator. It was sold to Essbee of Coatbridge in January 1995 and was sent to work in Campbeltown on a tendered service. It was re-sold in October 1995 and joined the fleet of Hutchison's of Overtown, where it would remain until May 2000. It then passed to John MacEwan and is seen here in Edinburgh. Moffat & Williamson acquired it in March 2004 and it would serve in Fife for around four and a half years before sale to Dent's of North Kelsey in December 2008.

W404 HOB was a Kassbohrer Setra S315GT-HD C48Ft purchased new by Anderson's of Castleford in August 2000. It passed to McCulloch's of Stranraer and was captured on a hire to Glasgow. The firm is based at Main Road, Stoneykirk, Stranraer, Wigtownshire.

A952 MNC was a Leyland Tiger TRCTL11/3R/LAG Galaxy C51Ft purchased new by Redfern of New Mills in February 1984. It passed to Specht of Forest Gate before purchase by Brownriggs of Thornhill in March 1994. It was re-registered to RLX 323 in January 1995 and remained in the fleet until April 2006, when it passed to Armstrong of Castle Douglas.

KKW 68P was a Leyland Leopard PSU3C/4R/Alexander Y Type DP49F purchased new by South Yorkshire PTE in March 1976. It was later put into the Compass Bus fleet at Wakefield, but on disposal it went to Burman Travel of Mile Oak, then MacEwan's of Dumfries. OSJ 618R was a similar bus, which had been new as Western SMT L2618 in January 1976. They were captured together in Dumfries.

KUM 508L was a Leyland Leopard PSU3B/4R/Plaxton Elite C53F purchased new by Hardwick's Services of Scarborough, which was a subsidiary of Wallace Arnold Tours of Leeds in March 1973. It passed to Nelson's of Thornhill, and was seen in Glasgow while working on a private hire.

TIB 403D was a DAF SB220CL/Hispano B51F that was new to TIBS, Singapore. It was imported to the UK and re-registered as G195 CLF by Capital of West Drayton for use at Heathrow Airport. It joined MacEwan's of Dumfries from Ashall of Clayton in April 2000, but was traded in to Arriva Bus and Coach (dealer) in May 2001, and later became a mobile bar.

PGA 833V was a Leyland Leopard PSU3F/4R/Alexander T Type C49F that was new to Central Scottish as their T393 in July 1980. It then passed to the merged Kelvin Central fleet, becoming 2533, before disposal to Gallagher of Waddington. It was acquired by John MacEwan in 2003 and received Dumfries & District livery. And is seen alongside LFJ 848W, an ex-Moffat & Williamson Bristol LH/ECW.

RHP 8R was a Volvo B58-56/Caetano Estoril C53F purchased new by Ron Bonas of Coventry in November 1976, and was also one of just fourteen that had this type of bodywork fitted to a Volvo B58 chassis. It was purchased by James King in 1988 from Clements of Nailsea and is seen on a football hire to Glasgow, but re-registered as PHU 253R. It had also been registered as 307 WHT at one time, but soon moved to Armstrong's of Castle Douglas.

E11 6UTX was a Leyland Lynx LX112 B51F purchased new by Merthyr Tydfil (116) in July 1988. It joined McKindless of Wishaw in 2000 from Arriva Cymru. It had also worked in Yorkshire for West Riding Group subsidiaries Yorkshire Buses and South Yorkshire Road Transport. It passed to King's of Kirkcowan from Stephenson of Tholthorpe in March 2004 for school contracts and is seen at the depot while being prepared for service.

KOG 947P was a Leyland Leopard PSU3C/4R/Plaxton Elite C34F that was new to Bowen's of Birmingham in September 1975. It was up-seated to C53F on joining the Carruthers fleet and was the flagship for a number of years. This view sees it on a private hire to Glasgow. It would pass to Peacock's with the business later on.

W302 EYG was an Optare Solo M850 B23F purchased new by HAD of Shotts in July 2000. It subsequently passed to Doyle of Ripley before joining McCall's of Lockerbie Coaches and was working the Castle Douglas town service with the registration plate KLX 108.

C634 PSW was a MAN MT8.136/G.C. Smith C24F that was new in 1986 to Armstrong of Castle Douglas and is seen on a private hire to Glasgow. The rather strange bodywork was built in Loughborough.

K766 DAO was a Volvo B10M-55/Alexander PS Type B49F that was new as Cumberland number 766 in March 1993. It was one of several refurbished after being damaged by the floods in Carlisle. It spent its latter years with MacEwan of Dumfries and is seen here arriving in Edinburgh on the 101 service.

G934 MYG was a DAF SB220/Optare Delta B49F that was new to London Buses as DA6 in April 1990. It subsequently went to Westlink before coming to Scotland and was one of three acquired by Dart Buses of Paisley. After disposal this one went to work for King's of Kirkcowan, and was photographed resting in Newton Stewart.

NPM 312F was a Ford R192/Strachans Pacesaver DP45F purchased new by Woburn Garages of London, t/a Evan Evans, in March 1968. The firm was taken over by Wallace Arnold, who felt this style was too service-bus-like for hires and disposed of them all quite quickly. By 1973 it had worked for Barries of Balloch, Mullen of Glasgow, and Sutherland of Abernethy. It joined Carruthers in November 1973 and ran until November 1975, when it passed to Allander of Milngavie.

LWV 268P was a Leyland Leopard PSU3C/4R/Plaxton Supreme C47F that was new as Southdown number 1268 in March 1976. It passed to Rennie's of Dunfermline in July 1987 and was re-seated to C46F. Gibson's acquired it in December 1993 and it remained until 1999.

RLS 469T was a Ford R1014/Alexander Y Type B45F that was new as Alexander (Midland) number MT69 in January 1979. It was transferred to Strathtay Scottish as their number SF19 in June 1985. On disposal it passed to Kenmagra of Lithwail before joining the MacEwan fleet in September 1989. It was sold to Melville of Kirriemuir in October 1991. Happily, it has been preserved in Strathtay livery.

SNK 249M was a Bedford YRT/Plaxton Elite C53F purchased new by Pilcher of Chatham in October 1973. It passed to Richardson of Lockerbie and was snapped in Glasgow. Bedford was a brand of vehicle produced by Vauxhall Motors, which was ultimately owned by General Motors.

SJ60 GBF was an Optare Solo SR M960 B31F purchased new by John MacEwan of Amisfield in October 2010. It is seen here near Locharbriggs. On disposal it passed to Stuart's of Carluke for further service.

J228 OKX was an Iveco 59.12/Marshall C31 B29F that was built as a demonstrator for Iveco-Ford, Winsford, in May 1992. It is seen here being put through its paces by McCulloch's of Stoneyburn on the 501 service, bound for Dumfries.

BFJ 313L was a Bristol RELH6L/Plaxton Elite C46F that was new as Greenslades Tours number 313 in June 1973. It was sold to Nu-Venture of Aylesford, before reaching MacEwan's of Amisfield in January 1989. John MacEwan sold it to Alan Dickson of Dumfries in July 1989, and Alan sold it back to John MacEwan!

A80 WHS was a DAF SB2300/Plaxton C53F Paramount 3200 that was new to Barrie's of Balloch in June 1984. It passed to Peacock of Locharbriggs and was snapped in Glasgow while on hire to Scottish Citylink. Peacock's drastically reduced the fleet around 1989 after the loss of council contracts and advertised the fleet for sale. They struggled on until 1995, when the business passed to MacEwan's.

RSD 969R was a Seddon Pennine VII/Alexander Y Type C49F purchased new by Western SMT as their S2666 in June 1977. It was transferred to Clydeside Scottish in 1985, becoming number 913 in that fleet. It then became Midland Scottish MSE 30, before sale to Beaton's of Blantyre where it received this mock KCB livery. This winter shot was taken in Dumfries in 1992 as it prepares to do a run to Moniaive while with Nelson's of Thornhill.

C112 JCS was a Leyland Tiger TRCLXC/2RH/Duple 320 C49Ft that was new as Central Scottish C12 in April 1986. It passed to Kelvin Central Buses in 1989, then Western in 1990, then Clydeside in 1991. On disposal it joined Wellington & Horsmill of Kingsbridge before reaching MacEwan's in July 1994, and was caught in Stranraer.

UGB 16R was an AEC Reliance 6U3ZR/Plaxton Supreme C51F purchased new by Hutchison's of Overtown in April 1977. It only lasted until 1980 and was sold to Nithcree Distributors of Dumfries, with whom it is shown. In 1983 it passed to Jubilee of Stevenage, Holmes of Chesnut acquired it in March 1984, and it passed to MacEwan's of Dumfries in May 1987, Dickson's of Dumfries in July 1987, and then back to MacEwan's in July 1991.

CTM 411T was a Leyland Leopard PSU5C/4R/Duple Dominant II C50F purchased new by Guards of London in January 1979. It moved to Hollick of Goldington before purchase by Brownrigg's of Thornhill in April 1991. It would remain in the fleet until March 2002, when it was sold to Dodd, Snaith & Tilley of Hebdon Bridge.

X523 SHH was a Dennis Dart SLF/Alexander ALX200 purchased new by Dave Garnett of Lockerbie, t/a White Star, in September 2000, shown here loading in Moffat. It would pass to Stagecoach with the business as number 33077, and later passed to Powell's of Rotherham as their number 65.

AVS 300 was a Ford 570E/Duple C41F purchased new by Doig's Tours (Greenock) Ltd in April 1960. It passed to Carruthers of New Abbey in July 1962 and served for ten years. It passed to Murchison of Kyle of Lochalsh and lasted until 1975.

D69 TWM was a Volvo B10M-61/Duple 350 C55F purchased new by Ashton of St Helens in June 1987. It passed to Evans of Tregaron before purchase by Armstrong of Castle Douglas in 2000. It moved to Brownrigg's of Thornhill in April 2006 and ran for four years.

B428 MSW was a Van Hool T815 C49F purchased new by Gibson's in April 1985, and seen in Moffat. It was re-registered as HIL 8028 and remained until August 2002, when it passed to Morrison's of Whiteness. It returned to its original plate in 2006 and passed to Manning of Croom in Eire. It was given the Irish number 85-LK-1350.

LSE 919V was a Bedford YMT/Plaxton Supreme C53F purchased new by Mayne's of Buckie in April 1980. On disposal it passed to Nithcree Coaches of Dumfries, and is shown here in Glasgow. It moved to Dickson's of Dumfries in 1988 and became 347 8SM, and later JHH 989V.

UGB 16R was an AEC Reliance 6U3ZR/Plaxton Supreme C51F purchased new by Hutchison's of Overtown in April 1977. It joined Dickson's of Dumfries in July 1987 and is shown leaving Dumfries Whitesands on a local journey to Woodlands Estate.

SRW 789W was a Ford R1114/Plaxton Supreme C53F purchased new by David Grasby of Oxhill in June 1981. It passed to Stretton Travel, then Matthews of Cwmbran, before reaching Nelson's in January 1991, and is seen in Thornhill. It would remain until September 1994, when it passed to Dalybus of Eccles.

F251 DKG was a Freight Rover F405D/Carlyle C2 B20F that was new as National Welsh number 251 in June 1989. On disposal it passed to Ambassador of Knutsford before purchase by Houston's of Lockerbie in May 1993. It was seen passing through Dumfries on service 117, bound for Dalton.

KUX 216W was a Leyland Leopard PSU5D/4R/Duple Dominant III C53F that was new as Whittle of Highley number 16 in November 1980. On disposal it passed to Oare's of Holywell before purchase by John MacEwan in February 1991, and is shown parked up at Amisfield. It moved to McCulloch's of Stoneykirk, near Stranraer, in February 1992.

TBC 578R was a Bedford YMT/Caetano C53F purchased new by Wainfleet of Nuneaton in May 1977. It later became ESU 308 with Butler's of Mitcham before purchase by Steele's in February 1982. It was parked outside the old Western SMT depot in Lockerbie that served as the company's garage.

VVK 200Y was a Van Hool T815 C49Ft purchased new by Fulton of Langley Park in June 1983. It moved to Watson's of Annfield Plain in January 1985 before reaching Beaton's of Blantyre in March 1988 and getting re-registered as LIB 5441 the following year. It was acquired by Gibson's of Moffat in July 1990 and remained until March 2003, when it passed to Whitestar of Neilston.

BX61 DXF was a Volvo B9R/Jonckheere SHV C53Ft purchased new by Reynolds Diplomat of Watford in September 2011. It joined Houston's of Lockerbie in 2016, and is seen in Glasgow on a football hire.

SWESTRANS livery is carried on this Mercedes Sprinter, which was running on service 385 bound for Annan. RJ65 WZK was operated by Houston's of Lockerbie, and was caught leaving the Loreburn Centre in Dumfries.

LUA 278V was a Leyland Leopard PSU3F/4R/Plaxton Supreme C46F purchased new by Wallace Arnold subsidiary Evan Evans of London in May 1980. It passed to James King of Kirkcowan, and was on a visit to the World Pipe Band Championships at Bellahouston Park in Glasgow.

CYD 724C was an AEC Reliance 2MU4R/Harrington Grenadier C41F purchased new by Hutchings & Cornelius of South Petherton in July 1965. It is shown here while with Andy McCall of Lockerbie in 1994. It would later pass to Rexquote of Bishops Lydeard.

LHL 247P was a Leyland Leopard PSU3C/4R/Alexander T Type C49F that was originally ordered by West Riding, but was delivered as Yorkshire Traction number 247 in May 1976. It was purchased by Peacock of Locharbriggs in 1986, and is seen in Dumfries, fitted with bus seats.

OJY 573S was a Volvo B58-61 / Plaxton Viewmaster C50F purchased new by Trathen's of Yelverton in April 1978. On disposal it passed to Mayer's of Manchester before purchase by Gibson's in 1983. The Viewmaster was a taller version of the Supreme III or IV, with the height increased by approximately 10 inches. The windscreen was a taller version of that used on the Supreme III and was retained unaltered for the Viewmaster IV. Both were also available to 'Express' specification, as the Viewmaster Express and Viewmaster IV Express respectively.

N504 LUA was a DAF SB3000/Ikarus Blue Danube C53F purchased new by London Coaches (Kent) in June 1996. It joined MacEwan's in June 2001, and was caught passing through Edinburgh. It would remain until June 2004, when it passed to Wealdon Omnibuses (dealer). Prentice Westwood later ran it as UO 6929.

B531 LSG was a Leyland Tiger TRCTL11/3RH/Alexander TC Type C53F purchased new by Silver Coach Lines of Edinburgh in April 1985, and was later re-registered as GSU 378. On disposal it passed to Docherty of Auchterarder, and became B734 XES, but arrived at Anderson's from Chalkwell of Sittingbourne as VIB 5240.

M996 CYS was a Mercedes 811D/Wadham Stringer B33F new as Pathfinder of Newark number 15 in September 1994. It passed to R. K. Armstrong of Castle Douglas, and was working on shuttles to the Wickerman music festival held in Dundrennan. It was resting between runs in Kirkcudbright.

UUL 652F was an AEC Reliance 6U3ZR/Plaxton Panorama C44F purchased new by Surrey Motors of Sutton as their number 60 in 1968. It passed to Brownrigg's of Thornhill and later ran for Alan Dickson of Dumfries in 1989 for a spell.

JNV 628Y was a Volvo B10M-61/Jonckheere Bermuda C49Ft purchased new by Volvoverland of Leeds in September 1982. On disposal it passed to Pettigrew's of Mauchline, where it was re-registered as 877 COT, before reaching Alan Dickson in June 1990. It was snapped on a visit to Glasgow, but was resold to King's of Kirkcowan in July 1991.

V973 DRM was Dennis Dart SLF/Plaxton Pointer B29F purchased new by Dave Garnett, t/a White Star of Lockerbie in January 2000. The business was purchased by Stagecoach North West, but later some of it was transferred to Stagecoach Western, including this bus, which was numbered as 33073. On disposal it joined Arthur's Coaches of Coatbridge, but that was still a long way off when this view was taken in Lockerbie when it was still new.

NLD 8V was a Leyland Leopard PSU5C/4R/Duple Dominant II C57F purchased new by Fox of Hayes as their number 69 in May 1980. It later ran for Proctor of Hanley, Chase Coaches and Letham of Blantyre before joining Nelson's of Thornhill in April 1992. It was loading at Dumfries Whitesands on the service to Cumnock.

VUD 29X was a Leyland Leopard PSU3G/4R/ECW C49F that was new as City of Oxford number 29 in April 1982. On disposal it passed to Fitzcharles of Grangemouth before purchase by MacEwan's in December 1993. It was unloading at Dumfries Whitesands. Eastern Coachworks built their bodywork in Lowestoft, but sadly closed down in January 1987.

125 MTE was a Leyland Tiger Cub PSUC1/2/Northern Counties C41F that was new as Lancashire United number 32 in 1960. It passed to Stokes of Carstairs in November 1970 and was re-seated with forty-five bus seats. It joined Leith's of Sanquhar in November 1977 and ran until April 1979.

P152 KSM was a Mercedes Benz 0405/Optare Prisma B47F purchased new by John MacEwan of Amisfield in October 1996. It was used on the Borders Rail-Link contract and was photographed in Hawick while bound for Galashiels. On disposal it was snapped up by East Yorkshire as their fleet number 248 before joining Mikes Travel as their number 29.

F550 TMH was a Volvo B10M-60/Van Hool Alizee C53F purchased new by Travellers of Hounslow in March 1989. On disposal in 1994 it passed to Glen Coaches of Port Glasgow. It joined the King of Kirkcowan fleet in 1998, and was passing through Ayr when snapped.

YJ15 APU was an Optare Solo M890SR B27F that was new in April 2015 and operated by Stagecoach Western as their fleet number 47916. It was in fact owned by SWESTRANS and re-allocated to Houston's of Lockerbie after tender changes in the area.

FY02 OTS was a Mercedes 614D/Autobus Classique C24F purchased new by Irvine's of Glenluce in 2002. It was loading in Stranraer for the 411 local service. Optare acquired Autobus Classique in 1996, shortly after the launch of their Nouvelle luxury minicoach. They significantly redesigned and rebadged it in 1997 as the Nouvelle 2, and it served similar markets to the StarRider and MetroRider coach versions.

JNV 628Y was a Volvo B10M-61/Jonckheere Bermuda C49Ft purchased new by Volvoverland of Leeds in September 1982. On disposal it passed to Pettigrew's of Mauchline, where it was re-registered as 877 COT, before reaching Alan Dickson in June 1990. It moved to King's of Kirkcowan in July 1991 and was snapped on a visit to Glasgow.

Ten Volvo B10Ms passed to John MacEwan in 2005. They had been caught in the Carlisle floods and were written off by the insurance company. They were refurbished and some were sold on, but others were used in service. K766 DAO is seen in Dumfries as it crossed the River Nith.

GFA 955 was a Van Hool Acron T815 C53Ft purchased new by Paterson's of Dalry in December 1984. It passed to McCulloch's of Stranraer in 1996, and was caught passing through Ayr town centre. On disposal it became B470 FCS. Most of the buses and coaches are built totally by Van Hool, with engines and axles sourced from Caterpillar, Cummins, DAF and MAN and gearboxes from ZF or Voith.

HVY 133X was a Bedford YMP/Plaxton Supreme C33F that was new as York Pullman number 133 in June 1982. It passed to Glenhire of Dyce before reaching King's of Kirkcowan, and was snapped in Bellahouston Park in Glasgow.

MCH 513W was a Ford R1114/Duple Dominant II C50F purchased new by Smith of Beeston in September 1980. It passed to McCulloch's of Stranraer, and was seen on a visit to Glasgow. In the Ford R1114, the R meant 'R series', the 11 referred to the length, i.e. 11 meters long, and the 14 referred to the 140 bhp engine fitted.

MK63 XAV is an ADL Enviro 200 B37F seen in Dumfries on service 372 from Sandyhills. The first generation Enviro200, then known as the TransBus Enviro200, was unveiled at Coach & Bus 2003 by the vehicle's then manufacturer TransBus International. Following the collapse of TransBus, the Enviro200 was rebranded as the Alexander Dennis Enviro200 by Alexander Dennis.

A selection of Peacock vehicles sit at the Whitesands in Dumfries. A pair of Alexander bodies flank Bristol LH CLJ 413Y. This was the last LH registered and was believed to have been a cancelled order from Harvey of Mousehole, which was taken by Bere Regis & District instead. It survives in preservation in BR&D livery.

F792 PSL was Sanos Charisma S315.21 C53F – a cheap 0303 that was built under licence in Yugoslavia. It had started life as F758 SPU and was new to Clarke & Ellwood of Chatteris in May 1989. It has carried various registrations, including GBZ 4991 and PIL 7617. It was purchased by Steele's Coaches (1996) Ltd from MacTavish of Dalmuir in July 1998, and was snapped in Glasgow.

DSV 711 was a Volvo B10M-61/Berkhof Esprite C49Ft purchased new by Wallace Arnold Tours, Devon, in March 1985. On disposal in January 1992 it passed to Royston Coaches before reaching Gibson's in June 1994. It was re-seated to C53F in April 2003, when it was sold to Moseley (dealer). It was re-registered to B588 FCS and passed to Causeway Coaches, St Margarets Hope, and ran until 2008. Sadly, Gibson's ceased trading on 14 November 2007.

TSW 8T was a Ford R1114/Duple Dominant II C49F that was new to Little's in March 1979. It was on a hire to Glasgow's Bellahouston Park during the World Pipe Band Championships. It was doing a hire for the Antrim Pipe Band, taking them to Stranraer for the ferry home. It would later serve with HAD Coaches of Shotts.

LUP 744J was an AEC Reliance 6MU3R/Plaxton Elite C53F purchased new by OK Motor Services of Bishop Auckland in January 1971. On disposal it joined Blair & Palmer of Carlisle, before reaching Richardson's of Lockerbie, and was captured on a visit to Hampden Park in Glasgow.

SA51 ZJN was a Volvo B10M-62/Caetano Enigma C51Ft purchased new by Cuthbert of Annan, t/a Oor Coaches. It was passing through Edinburgh while working on an Urquhart tour. The roots of Caetano Coachbuilders can be traced back to 1946, when Salvador Fernandes Caetano started Portugal's first coachbuilding firm under the name Martins, Caetano & Irmão.

OYS 173M was a Leyland Atlantean AN68/1R/Alexander AL Type H76F purchased new by Greater Glasgow PTE as their LA776 in February 1974. It passed to Strathclyde Buses and was disposed of in June 1988 to Rennie's of Dunfermline. It is seen here with Alan Dickson of Dumfries. I just love the way they kept the 'dummy' window, which was originally part of an advert. It was sold later to Wilson's of Carnwath for spares.

EGA 832C was a Bedford VAS1/Willowbrook B29F purchased new by David MacBrayne of Glasgow as their fleet number 97 in May 1965. It passed to Highland Omnibuses as CD79 in November 1971, and joined Carruthers in February 1974, giving around four years of service. It was captured at Dumfries Whitesands. The original Carruthers livery had been blue, but this was changed in 1929 to the familiar brown and yellow, which was copied from a Minerva demonstrator. The business was sold to Peacock (Truck Services) in December 1983.

RGS 95R was an AEC Reliance 6U3ZR/Plaxton Supreme C57F purchased new by Rowson Brothers of Hayes in March 1977. It then passed to Stewart's, t/a Aberfeldy Coaches, before reaching John MacEwan of Dumfries in July 1990. It then joined David Bowman's fleet at Burthwaite for further service.

ACS 42T was a Leyland Leopard PSU3E/4R/Plaxton Supreme C53F purchased new by Clyde Coast Co-operative member McGregor of Saltcoats in April 1979. Gibsons bought it from Clyde Coast in March 1987 and it is seen at Dumfries Whitesands, having just arrived from Ae village. Sadly, Gibson's ceased business on 21 November 2007.

Leith of Sanquhar used various liveries over the years, with this scheme copied from a MacRae of Hamilton coach. PCK 149P was a Leyland Leopard PSU3C/4R/Duple Dominant C47F that was new as National Travel (North West) number 149 in March 1976, while PSB 2S was a Ford R1114/Plaxton Supreme C53F that was new to Gorman's of Dunoon in July 1977.

L26 LSG was a Mercedes 709D/Alexander (Belfast) B25F purchased new by Bryans of Denny in December 1993. It passed to Southern National as their number 743 before joining Houston's of Lockerbie. It would later work for City Sprinter of Glasgow and McNairn's of Coatbridge.

BVA 787V was a Leyland Leopard PSU3F/5R/Plaxton Supreme C49F that was new as Premier Travel number 285 in April 1980. It passed to Green's of Kirkintilloch and Beaton's of Blantyre before joining Nelson's of Thornhill in February 1992. It then moved to Warner's of Tewkesbury in September 1994 and ran as LIL 3066 with the Boomerang Bus Company.

JLS 725S was a Leyland Leopard PSU3E/4R/Duple Dominant C49F purchased new by Alexander (Midland) as their MPE312 in May 1978. It was transferred to Kelvin Scottish as their 3029 in June 1985. It passed to Davis of Bridport before purchase by MacEwan's of Dumfries in January 1989; however it soon moved to Dickson's of Dumfries.

SN15 LRX is an ADL Enviro E20D B39F purchased new by Houston's of Lockerbie in May 2015, and seen loading for Annan on service 383. Alexander Dennis is a British bus-building company based in Scotland and is the largest bus and coach manufacturer in the United Kingdom. In early 2016, Alexander Dennis had a 44 per cent market share in the United Kingdom, and at April 2014, Brian Souter and Ann Gloag collectively held a 55 per cent shareholding.

OOS 923V was a Bedford YMT/Plaxton Supreme C53F purchased new by James King of Kirkcowan in June 1980, seen here on a hire to Glasgow. It would later run for Rogers of Graigfechan.

YSN 959K was a Ford R192/Plaxton Derwent DP45F purchased new by Green's of Kirkintilloch in November 1971. It passed to Currian Road Tours of Nanpean in March 1975 before reaching Carruthers in January 1977. It passed with the business to Peacocks in December 1983 and later to Steele of Dumfries and Bruce of Longtown. It was seen resting between duties at Dumfries Whitesands.

MV02 UMD was a Volvo B12M-62/Van Hool C46Ft purchased new by Shearings Holidays (404) in March 2002, and joined McDade's of Uddingston in August 2012. It became SIL 1075 in 2013, but has now returned to its original plate with Andy McCall. It has received fleet livery and is a credit to its owner, as shown in this view taken in Dumfries. It later became PJI 3746.

WCK 129V was a Leyland Leopard PSU3E/4R/Duple Dominant II C49F purchased new by Ribble (1129) in November 1979. It was transferred to Cumberland in February 1986. On disposal it passed to Nord-Anglia International of Southport in June 1988, moving to Holmwood Coaches in December 1988. By January 1992 it was with Safeways Travel of Blackpool, and joined Gibson's in December 1993. It lasted for seven years before withdrawal in January 2000 and was sold to Dunsmore (dealer) of Larkhall two months later.

OOX 810R was a Leyland National 11351A/1R B50F that was new as West Midlands PTE number 6810 in May 1977. It spent time on hire to North Western and Arriva North West before being purchased by John MacEwan in June 2001, and was seen in Dumfries.

The flags were out today for Houston's MX10 DXS. This Optare Solo was purchased new in April 2010, and was caught in its home town. Much of Lockerbie is built from red sandstone. There are several imposing buildings near the centre – none more so than the Town Hall, finished in 1880, complete with its clock tower.

SRS 134 was a Bedford VAS1/Willowbrook B30F that was new as Alexander (Northern) number NW 264 in May 1962. Carruthers purchased it from S&N Motors (dealer) in December 1971 and ran it until June 1976, when it passed to a local builders.

JVW 156Y was a Volvo B10M-61/Berkhof Everest C49Ft purchased new by Contractus of Stevenage in March 1983. The following year it passed to Charter Coach of Great Oakley, later becoming Smith of Rayne number 26. It was acquired by McCulloch of Stranraer in 1992 and was caught passing through Glasgow.

YX08 MHZ is a Plaxton Primo EB03 B28F first registered by Plaxtons of Scarborough in July 2008. It has worked for Bakerbus and Creigiau Travel before arriving with McCall's of Lockerbie. The model was launched by Plaxton in 2005 and was the result of close co-operation between Enterprise Bus Ltd (the chassis manufacturer) and Plaxton. The fully welded stainless steel integral chassis final assembly was supplied in right-hand-drive format as a running unit to Plaxton. Final body assembly was undertaken by Plaxton in Scarborough.

R50 TPB was a Bova FHD12-340 C49Ft purchased new by Thomas Paterson & Brown of Dalry in November 1997. It passed to Gibson's of Moffat in March 2003, and was parked at Moffat Woollen Mill. It left the fleet in April 2006, passing to Cedric's of Wivenhoe as FSK 868.

ML62 OHB was a Neoplan N2216/3 C49Ft purchased new by Ellison of St Helens in November 2012. Houston's were visiting Aberdeen with a party from Dalbeattie Star F. C. In 2001 Neoplan was acquired by MAN AG. A new coach designed for touring was introduced in 2003 under the name Tourliner.

FSW 40Y was a Leyland Tiger TRCTL11/3R/Plaxton Paramount 3500 C51F that was delivered new to Little's in May 1983 and was photographed at Glasgow's Bellahouston Park. The Plaxton Paramount coach first appeared at the 1982 British Motor Show and was built until 1992 in Scarborough. The '3500' refers to the height in millimetres.

YP02 AAY was a Scania L94UB/Wright B43F that was new as Rapson's number 210 in March 2002. It joined MacEwan's in June 2003, and was caught in Edinburgh. It moved on to Harrogate Coach Travel in January 2015.